PAN AFRICAN LIFESTYLE

DIGITAL DOMINANCE AFRICA

How African Creators Build Audiences, Monetize Their Work & Thrive Independently

EMMANUEL BOPE *and* SOLANGE BOPE

Authors: Emmanuel Bope and Solange Bope

Printed and bound in Canada

First printing February 2026

Published by PAN AFRICAN LIFESTYLE Inc.

Calgary, Alberta

978-1-998780-89-1 Softcover

www.panafricanlifestyle.com

A portion of the proceeds from this book is allocated to empower African creatives through initiatives by Pan African Lifestyle Inc. Thank you for supporting Afrifluencers in the motherland.

DEDICATION

*We begin by giving thanks to **God Most High**, the Creator, for the wisdom, vision, and guidance that have made this work possible. It is through His provision that we are able to dream, create, and build frameworks that elevate Africa's digital future.*

This book is dedicated to every African creator, entrepreneur, innovator, and institution striving to build influence, authority, and sustainable systems in the digital space. To those who see beyond fleeting attention and understand that true impact is measured by real revenue, operational systems, and enduring legacy, this is for you.

To the African diaspora and all partners investing talent, knowledge, and capital into the continent, your commitment strengthens the bridge between vision and reality.

Finally, to the next generation of African digital architects, creators, and institutional leaders: may this book inspire and equip you to claim your space online, build professional systems, and design the African digital century with purpose, excellence, and integrity.

Emmanuel & Solange

CONTENTS

Dedication — 8
Table of Contents — 10
Disclaimer — 13
Preface — 15
Introduction — 18
Opportunity in Africa — 19
Beyond Virality — 20
Defining Roles: Creator, Architect, Operator — 20

Part I: Identity and Influence — 22
African Culture & Community Connection — 23
The Digital Ecosystem — 23
Regional Tech Trends — 24
Cultural Relevance — 24
African Digital Identity — 24
Defining Presence — 25
Credibility Online — 25
Creators vs. Content Businesses — 25
Hobbyists vs. Professionals — 26
The Digital African Citizen — 26
Civic Participation — 26
Digital Ethics — 27

Part II: The Foundation of Digital Authority — 29
Storytelling for Influence — 29
Cultural Narratives — 30
Pan-African Digital Thought — 31
Content Architecture — 31
Establishing Authority — 32

Community & Trust Building — 32
Authority vs. Popularity — 33
Measuring Credibility — 33
Defining Value Online — 34

Part III: Attention, Strategy & Impact — 35
Why Attention Matters — 35
Content Strategy — 35
Narrative Power & Impact — 35
Storytelling for Change — 36
Audience Selection — 37
Platform Strategy — 37
Cross-Platform Growth — 38
Structuring Engagement — 38
Beyond Vanity Metrics — 38

Part IV: Revenue & Sustainability — 40
Monetization Strategies — 40
Creator vs. Digital Business — 41
Building Media Companies — 41
Digital Products & Services — 42
Diaspora Monetization Opportunities — 42
Strategic Partnerships — 43
Case Studies — 43
Case Study: System in Action — 44
Pan-African Lifestyle: From Cultural Ideas to Structural Multimedia Infrastructure — 44
From Viral Moment to Continental Authority — 45
African Stream: Platform Vulnerability & the Sovereignty Imperative — 46
IShowSpeed: Narrative Disruption at Global Scale — 47
Composite Case Study: The Creator Who Went Viral but Stayed Broke — 47
Composite Case Study: The Diaspora Bridge Model — 48

Composite Case Study: Operator Survived Deplatforming — 48
Composite Case Study: From Creator to Institution — 49

Part V: From Dependency to Sovereignty — 50
Owning the Platform — 50
Platform & Data Control — 51
Self-Reliant Systems — 51
Protecting the Continent — 52
Cybersecurity — 52
Standards for Trust — 52
Professional Standards — 53
Transparency & Accountability — 53
Scaling Influence — 53

Part VI: Institutional & Personal Impact — 55
Institutional Influence — 55
Campaigns for Governments & Corporations — 56
Public-Private Partnerships — 56
The Entrepreneurial State & Private Sector — 57
Financing the Digital Century — 57
Investment Models — 57
Governance & Standards — 58
Measuring Influence & Impact — 58
KPIs for Digital Authorities — 58
Phased Implementation: 2030, 2040, 2050 — 59
Step-by-Step Roadmap — 59

Lessons Learned — 60
Conclusion — 64
Appendices — 67
Appendix A — 67
Appendix B — 68
Appendix C — 68
Acknowledgments — 70
Author Bio — 76

DISCLAIMER

The content of this book is provided for informational and educational purposes only. While every effort has been made to ensure the accuracy and reliability of the information presented, the authors, contributors, and publishers do not assume any responsibility or liability for errors, omissions, or outcomes resulting from the application of the ideas and strategies contained herein.

This book outlines concepts, frameworks, and practices designed to guide individuals, businesses, and institutions in building influence, authority, and digital systems in Africa. Readers are encouraged to exercise their own judgment, conduct due diligence, and seek professional advice where appropriate before implementing any strategies or making financial, legal, or business decisions.

The mention of any product, service, platform, or organization does not constitute an endorsement. Likewise, the absence of reference to any specific entity should not be interpreted as a negative judgment.

By reading this book, you acknowledge that success in digital influence, business, or institutional systems requires effort, strategic thinking, and consistent execution. The authors and publishers make no guarantees regarding financial results, growth, or outcomes.

PREFACE

Africa is entering a moment of unprecedented opportunity. The continent is no longer merely a consumer of global digital trends. It is becoming a space where influence, innovation, and authority can be built, owned, and scaled by Africans for Africans. This book is written for those who are ready to claim that space.

Digital dominance is more than viral content or online popularity. It is a deliberate, disciplined approach to building influence, generating revenue, and establishing sustainable systems. It is about transforming personal, business, and institutional presence into professional authority that lasts. The strategies, frameworks, and insights presented in this book are designed to guide creators, entrepreneurs, institutions, and governments in achieving measurable, long-term impact.

This book also challenges misconceptions about what it means to be a digital professional. A content creator who earns no revenue or builds no system is not the same as a digital architect or a content business operator. Here, we define the standards for professional legitimacy, responsibility, and success. We outline how individuals and institutions can move from casual participation online to structured influence and authority, creating systems that support both personal growth and continental development.

The vision of **Digital Dominance Africa** is bold. It is not about fleeting trends or short-term attention. It is about ownership—of platforms, data, narratives, and systems. It is about building a digital infrastructure that empowers Africans to control their story, their economy, and their future.

This book is both a roadmap and a call to action. It is a guide for anyone ready to invest in themselves, their communities, and the continent. It is a reference for building sustainable digital businesses, professional institutions, and networks that amplify African voices. It is a blueprint for shaping the African digital century.

We invite you to read, reflect, and act. The frameworks in this book are tested and designed to work across individuals, organizations, and institutions. They are not abstract ideas but practical strategies for those committed to building influence, authority, and professional systems that will define Africa's digital future.

The time is now. Africa's digital century is not approaching—it has already begun. This book is your guide to participating fully, building responsibly, and leading with purpose.

INTRODUCTION

AFRICA'S DIGITAL CENTURY

Africa stands at the threshold of a transformative digital era. The continent is no longer simply a participant in global digital trends. It is a space of enormous opportunity, where influence, creativity, and systems can be built, owned, and scaled by Africans. The choices made today will determine whether this generation converts potential into enduring power. But opportunity alone does not guarantee dominance.

Across the continent, creators are building audiences, producing content, and generating visibility at unprecedented levels. Yet visibility does not automatically translate into ownership. Engagement does not automatically translate into revenue. Influence does not automatically translate into independence.

Many African creators operate within global digital systems that were not designed with African economic realities in mind. Monetization structures are uneven. Payment access can be limited. Revenue distribution varies by geography.

Brand ecosystems are still developing. Infrastructure costs remain high relative to income. As a result, many can attract attention. Far fewer can convert that attention into sustainable, scalable digital businesses. This book addresses that gap.

Opportunity in Africa

The opportunities are unprecedented. Africa's people, culture, knowledge, and networks—both on the continent and in the diaspora—are unmatched resources. Demographic momentum, mobile-first adoption, and expanding connectivity create the foundation for a powerful digital economy.

But digital attention alone is not enough. Popularity without structure is temporary. Visibility without monetization is fragile. Influence without systems is vulnerable. True digital dominance requires converting engagement into measurable outcomes, ideas into infrastructure, and creativity into professional authority and revenue. The question is no longer whether Africa can participate in the digital economy. The question is whether African creators will own their position within it.

Beyond Virality

Success in the African digital century is not about chasing trends or accumulating temporary attention. Virality is not a strategy. It is a moment. Sustainable success requires authority that compounds, systems that scale, revenue that is diversified, and infrastructure that is owned. Influence must be deliberate, structured, and economically grounded. It must translate into professional growth, financial sustainability, and long-term legacy. This book moves beyond the pursuit of attention. It focuses on building systems that convert attention into independence.

Defining Roles: Creator, Architect, Operator

To participate meaningfully, it is essential to understand the distinction between roles. The Creator attracts attention and builds visibility. The Architect designs the systems—content models, platforms, workflows, and monetization pathways—that transform visibility into structured influence. The Operator scales those systems to produce revenue, institutional credibility, and measurable impact across communities, markets, and sectors. Many remain at the Creator level. Few evolve into Architects. Even fewer become Operators.

Digital dominance requires movement through all three stages. This book introduces structured frameworks to guide that evolution: how to build authority that commands trust, how to engineer attention strategically, how to monetize without dependency, and how to build infrastructure that protects ownership. The African digital century is not a trend. It is a generational shift.

This book provides the roadmap to build influence responsibly, professionally, and independently—creating platforms, networks, and systems by Africans, for Africans. Influence without ownership is fleeting. Visibility without structure is unstable. Attention without monetization is fragile. The time to build with discipline and long-term vision is now.

PART I

THE AFRICAN DIGITAL REALITY

Identity and Influence

Digital influence in Africa cannot be separated from identity. In many parts of the world, online identity is fragmented or purely individualistic. In the African context, identity is layered. It is personal, cultural, communal, and historical at the same time. This creates both strength and complexity. African creators do not speak into a vacuum. They speak into living cultures, intergenerational narratives, evolving economies, and highly relational communities. Influence is not simply about visibility; it is about credibility within context. An audience may follow you because you are entertaining, but they trust you because you are culturally aligned. Authority in the African digital space is not built solely on performance. It is built on resonance. To build sustainable influence, creators must understand who they are representing, who they are serving, and what responsibility accompanies visibility. Influence detached from identity is unstable. Influence grounded in identity compounds.

Africa: Culture, Community, Connection

Community is not a marketing tactic in Africa. It is a lived reality. Digital growth strategies imported from highly individualistic markets often emphasize personal branding above all else. While personal branding matters, African audiences respond strongly to collective identity, shared progress, and communal advancement. This is an advantage. Where algorithm-driven cultures prioritize speed and novelty, African digital communities often prioritize relational trust and shared values. Creators who understand this can build deeper loyalty, stronger engagement, and more sustainable ecosystems. Connection is currency, but connection must be intentional.

Digital Ecosystems

Africa's digital ecosystem is not uniform. Connectivity rates vary. Payment systems vary. Platform access varies. Brand maturity varies. Infrastructure costs vary. This unevenness creates friction, but it also creates opportunity. In emerging ecosystems, early builders often define standards. Creators who understand the infrastructure they are operating within can design smarter systems. Instead of reacting emotionally to platform limitations, disciplined creators engineer around them. Digital ecosystems reward those who understand the terrain.

Regional Tech Trends

Mobile-first usage dominates. Short-form content adoption continues to expand. E-commerce integration is accelerating. Digital payment innovation is growing. Diaspora engagement remains strong. These trends create structural advantages for creators who think beyond content and into systems. The African digital environment may not mirror Western development patterns, but it does not need to. Different does not mean inferior. It means strategic adaptation is required.

Cultural Relevance

Relevance is not about imitation. Many creators make the mistake of copying global trends without contextual adaptation. This can generate temporary engagement but rarely produce lasting authority. Cultural fluency matters. Content that reflects lived realities, shared humor, economic context, and social aspirations resonates more deeply than generic trend participation. The strongest digital brands understand how to translate global frameworks into local relevance without losing authenticity. Relevance is leverage.

African Digital Identity

Digital identity is not simply a username and a logo. It is positioning, narrative, and alignment. African creators must decide early whether they are building entertainment brands, educational platforms, professional authority, community movements, or commercial enterprises. Clarity of identity determines clarity of monetization. Confusion at the identity level leads to instability at the revenue level. Identity precedes infrastructure.

Defining Presence

Presence is more than frequency. It is coherence. A strong digital presence has clear positioning, consistent messaging, recognizable tone, and defined value. Without clarity of presence, growth becomes random. With clarity of presence, growth becomes intentional. Presence is the foundation upon which systems are built.

Credibility Online

Credibility is fragile in digital environments. African creators face a dual challenge. They must establish trust within their communities while also competing in a global digital marketplace. Credibility is built through consistency, demonstrated expertise, transparent communication, and delivering measurable value. Attention may come quickly. Trust takes time. Long-term digital dominance requires both.

Creator vs. Content Business

There is a difference between being a creator and running a content business. A creator produces content.

A content business produces revenue. Many African creators build large followings without building monetization infrastructure. They operate at the level of visibility rather than sustainability. To thrive independently, visibility must convert into structured income streams. The shift from creator to content business is not cosmetic. It is structural.

Hobbyist vs. Professional

The African digital environment is maturing. What was once experimental is now economic. Hobbyists create when inspired. Professionals create with strategy. Hobbyists measure likes. Professionals measure revenue, retention, conversion, and lifetime value. The difference is not talent. It is discipline. Digital dominance requires professional standards.

Digital African Citizen

Digital participation is no longer optional. African creators are not only entertainers or entrepreneurs. They are digital citizens shaping discourse, influencing markets, and impacting institutions. With visibility comes responsibility. Civic participation, economic literacy, and ethical clarity matter in digital spaces. Influence without responsibility destabilizes ecosystems. Influence with discipline strengthens them.

Civic Participation

Creators increasingly influence public conversations. They shape narratives around governance, entrepreneurship, education, technology, and culture. Understanding the power of narrative is critical. Narrative shapes perception. Perception shapes markets. Markets shape opportunity. Digital creators are participants in continental development conversations, whether they recognize it or not.

Digital Ethics

As ecosystems grow, ethical standards must rise. Monetization pressure can encourage misinformation, manipulative marketing, short-term exploitation, and audience fatigue. Sustainable digital power requires ethical discipline. Trust is the ultimate long-term asset. Without it, systems collapse. With it, influence compounds. Part I defines the terrain. It clarifies the structural realities, advantages, and responsibilities of operating in Africa's digital environment. From here, visibility must evolve into authority.

Digital participation is no longer optional. It is structural. The African digital landscape is complex, uneven, and rapidly evolving, but it rewards those who understand context before ambition. Before chasing visibility, builders must understand identity. Before monetizing, they must understand ecosystem. Those who master the terrain gain leverage. Those who ignore it remain reactive. The next stage is not about more content. It is about more control.

PART II

THE AFRICAN CREATOR POWER STACK™

The Foundation of Digital Authority

Sustainable digital dominance does not begin with attention. It begins with structure. Many creators attempt to grow first and organize later, but that sequence produces volatility. The African Creator Power Stack™ establishes internal alignment before external expansion. It builds authority before amplification and creates leverage before scale. The Power Stack™ is a structured progression that transforms creativity into credibility and credibility into economic power. It rests on layered development in which identity anchors authority, authority attracts community, community validates value, and value enables ownership. When these elements are built deliberately and in sequence, digital growth becomes stable rather than reactive. Without structure, influence collapses under pressure. With structure, influence compounds.

Storytelling for Influence

Influence begins with narrative clarity. Before algorithms distribute content, stories establish meaning. In African contexts especially, narrative carries memory, continuity, and collective understanding. Digital creators who master storytelling do not simply inform or entertain; they shape perception. Effective storytelling positions the creator as a reliable interpreter of experience. It clarifies who the message serves, why it matters, and what shifts because of it. Storytelling aligned with strategic intent builds recognition, and recognition builds trust. Trust, sustained over time, evolves into authority. Without narrative discipline, content becomes noise. With narrative precision, influence becomes directional and measurable.

Cultural Narratives

Every creator operates within cultural context, whether acknowledged or not. Cultural narratives influence what audiences trust, value, question, and aspire toward. Ignoring these narratives weakens positioning. Engaging them intelligently strengthens resonance. Cultural fluency allows creators to build relevance without imitation. It enables them to translate global ideas into locally meaningful frameworks and ensures that authority feels earned rather than imported. In emerging digital markets, relevance determines retention. Creators who understand cultural alignment convert attention into loyalty more effectively than those who replicate trends without contextual grounding.

Pan-African Digital Thought

Digital influence no longer operates within narrow geographic boundaries. African creators function within interconnected continental and diaspora networks. A disciplined creator understands that visibility can scale beyond immediate locality when positioned thoughtfully. Pan-African digital thought requires strategic awareness of shared identity, economic interconnection, and cross-border opportunity. It means designing content and systems with expansion in mind rather than limitation. When creators think beyond narrow assumptions, they build structures capable of scaling naturally. Influence expands when perspective expands.

Content Architecture

Creativity without architecture is inconsistent. Content architecture defines how ideas are organized, reinforced, and distributed across platforms. It determines whether audiences remember a brand or forget it. A disciplined content architecture clarifies thematic focus, reinforces positioning, aligns messaging with monetization pathways, and creates repetition without redundancy. This reduces randomness and increases predictability. Structured content produces structured growth. Architecture transforms effort into leverage and prevents creative energy from dissipating without measurable return.

Establishing Authority

Authority is not declared; it is demonstrated. It emerges through consistent delivery, visible competence, and measurable value. In the African digital environment, authority must balance cultural alignment with professional discipline. Audiences evaluate reliability before they invest attention long term. Authority grows when creators solve problems repeatedly, communicate clearly, and maintain strategic focus. Without authority, monetization remains fragile. With authority, opportunities multiply. Authority converts visibility into influence that carries economic weight.

Community and Trust Building

Community is not an audience count. It is a network of individuals who identify with a shared value proposition and repeatedly engage with it. Trust transforms passive followers into active participants. Trust develops through transparency, responsiveness, and consistent delivery over time. In relational digital cultures, trust reduces friction in transactions and strengthens loyalty. It increases retention, referrals, and long-term engagement. Community bridges influence and income. Without trust, revenue spikes temporarily and declines. With trust, monetization stabilizes and compounds.

Authority vs. Popularity

Popularity fluctuates, but authority compounds. Popularity is driven by trends and temporary attention cycles, while authority is built through clarity, credibility, and demonstrated expertise. Many creators prioritize visible metrics while neglecting the deeper work of positioning. Authority allows creators to charge premium rates, negotiate stronger partnerships, and influence decision-making beyond their immediate audience. Popularity may increase reach, but authority increases leverage. Sustainable digital dominance requires prioritizing credibility over applause.

Measuring Credibility

Metrics can mislead. High impressions do not guarantee trust, and engagement does not guarantee loyalty. Growth without retention indicates instability. Credibility must be evaluated through behavioral signals such as repeat engagement, direct inquiries, referrals, and measurable audience action. Disciplined creators assess performance based on long-term stability rather than short-term spikes. Measurement aligned with strategic objectives protects momentum and reinforces authority over time.

Defining Value Online

Value is the economic core of digital systems. Every creator must clearly define the transformation, solution, or experience they provide. Undefined value produces inconsistent income and confused positioning. Clear value attracts aligned audiences and strategic partners while simplifying pricing and monetization pathways. When value is explicit and measurable, transactions become ethical and sustainable. Value clarity completes the Power Stack™. Once identity, authority, and community are aligned, value can be delivered with confidence, and ownership becomes attainable.

The African Creator Power Stack™ ensures that influence is not accidental. It is engineered. It converts creativity into authority and authority into economic leverage.

Authority is not accidental. It is layered. Identity anchors positioning. Positioning builds credibility. Credibility attracts community. Community validates value. Value enables ownership. When these elements are aligned, influence becomes durable. The Power Stack™ is not theory. It is structure. Those who build it deliberately will not depend on trends to survive.

PART III

THE AFRICAN ATTENTION ENGINE™

Why Attention Matters

Attention is the entry point to opportunity. In digital environments, it determines visibility, partnership potential, pricing power, and institutional recognition. Yet attention alone has no value unless it is structured. Many creators confuse exposure with progress. They measure views and followers without asking whether those numbers translate into leverage. The African Attention Engine™ reframes attention as a strategic asset rather than a vanity metric. Attention must be aligned with authority, connected to value, and directed toward monetization pathways. When unmanaged, attention becomes distraction. When engineered, it becomes power.

Content Strategy

Content without strategy produces unpredictable results. A disciplined content strategy clarifies positioning, defines thematic focus, and aligns messaging with long-term objectives. Every piece of content should reinforce identity and move audiences closer to defined value. Random output generates temporary spikes. Structured output builds momentum. In emerging digital markets, consistency and clarity outperform chaos. Strategy ensures that growth is not accidental but intentional. It reduces emotional decision-making and replaces it with measurable progression.

Narrative Power and Impact

Narrative determines retention. In saturated digital spaces, information is abundant but coherence is rare. Creators who understand narrative structure hold attention longer and convert more effectively. A strong narrative connects message to meaning and meaning to consequence. It ensures that content is not consumed and forgotten but internalized and acted upon. Narrative power shapes perception. Perception shapes demand. Demand shapes revenue. When narrative is disciplined, attention compounds rather than disperses.

Storytelling for Change

Storytelling becomes transformative when it is aligned with direction. It clarifies what the audience should understand, question, or pursue differently. In professional, entrepreneurial, or educational contexts, storytelling strengthens positioning and deepens credibility. It connects abstract information to lived experience. When storytelling lacks purpose, it entertains temporarily. When it carries intention, it builds loyalty. Change-oriented storytelling moves audiences from passive observation to active participation.

Audience Selection

Audience size is not the primary indicator of influence. Audience alignment is. Attempting to speak to everyone dilutes positioning and weakens authority. A disciplined creator identifies who benefits most from their work and builds deliberately around that segment. In many African digital environments, focused communities generate stronger economic results than broad, disengaged followings. Depth creates stability. Clarity of audience simplifies messaging, strengthens conversion, and reduces wasted effort.

Platform Strategy

Platforms are distribution tools, not foundations. Algorithms evolve, monetization policies shift, and access conditions fluctuate. Relying entirely on a single platform introduces structural vulnerability. The African Attention Engine™ treats platforms as channels for amplification rather than anchors for identity. Strategic creators adapt to platform mechanics without surrendering ownership. They design systems that can function across environments. Flexibility protects growth from disruption.

Cross-Platform Growth

Cross-platform growth reinforces authority and reduces dependency. It ensures that attention is not confined to a single algorithmic ecosystem. Intelligent adaptation across channels strengthens brand recognition while preserving coherence. Cross-platform presence increases resilience. When one channel slows, others sustain momentum. This reduces volatility and protects revenue pathways. Sustainable growth is diversified growth.

Structuring Engagement

Engagement must move beyond interaction into participation. Likes and comments signal awareness, but deeper engagement signals trust. Structured engagement includes calls to action that guide audiences toward subscription, enrollment, inquiry, or purchase. It aligns content with measurable response. When engagement is structured, creators gain insight into audience intent. Superficial engagement produces noise. Intentional engagement produces conversion.

Beyond Vanity Metrics

Vanity metrics distort judgment. High impressions without retention create illusion. Sustainable attention must be measured through behavioral indicators such as repeat engagement, referral activity, direct outreach, and purchasing behavior. Growth that does not translate into stability is fragile. The African Attention Engine™ prioritizes metrics that indicate durability rather than spikes. When performance is evaluated correctly, decisions improve. When decisions improve, systems strengthen.

The African Attention Engine™ transforms attention from unpredictable exposure into controlled expansion. It ensures that visibility feeds authority rather than ego. When attention is engineered properly, it becomes predictable. When predictable, it becomes scalable. When scalable, it becomes monetizable. Now we move into the most critical section of the book.

Attention is not the goal. It is the gateway. Without direction, it distracts. Without alignment, it exhausts. When engineered with discipline, attention becomes predictable, measurable, and monetizable. The difference between noise and leverage is architecture. The next step is to convert attention into economic independence.

PART IV

MONETIZATION WITHOUT PERMISSION

Revenue and Sustainability

Revenue is the dividing line between influence and independence. Visibility without income produces dependency. Income without structure produces instability. Sustainable digital careers require deliberate monetization architecture. In many African markets, platform-based ad revenue alone is unreliable due to uneven monetization access, fluctuating payout rates, and currency disparities. Creators who rely exclusively on platform payouts remain vulnerable to policy shifts and algorithmic volatility. Monetization without permission means designing income streams that do not depend on a single gatekeeper. It prioritizes ownership, diversification, and control.

Monetization Strategies

Effective monetization begins with alignment. Revenue models must match audience needs, creator expertise, and market purchasing power. African creators often operate in mixed economies where audiences include local consumers with constrained spending power and diaspora audiences with higher purchasing capacity. Strategic monetization accounts for this diversity. Direct services, consulting, digital education, paid communities, partnerships, and productized expertise frequently generate more reliable income than ad-based payouts alone. Monetization becomes powerful when it is value-driven and structured rather than opportunistic.

Creator vs. Digital Business

There is a structural difference between generating income occasionally and operating a digital business. A creator earns when content performs. A digital business earns through systems. Systems include recurring offers, defined pricing structures, automated workflows, and clear value propositions. Without systems, revenue fluctuates unpredictably. With systems, revenue stabilizes. Transitioning from creator to business requires intentional design. It demands clarity around customer journey, offer positioning, and delivery infrastructure. Independence requires moving beyond transactional earnings into repeatable income models.

Building Media Companies

Individual creators can evolve into structured media entities. A media company does not require a large team or complex infrastructure at the beginning. It requires clear editorial direction, monetization pathways, and scalable distribution. Media entities generate income through sponsorships, partnerships, premium content, education products, and strategic collaborations. As authority strengthens, opportunities expand. Building a media company shifts perception from influencer to institution. That shift increases negotiating power and long-term valuation.

Digital Products and Services

Digital products provide scalable revenue potential. Educational courses, e-books, membership platforms, toolkits, templates, advisory sessions, and specialized training programs allow creators to monetize expertise directly. Services such as consulting, strategy development, coaching, and campaign advisory provide higher-ticket opportunities. African creators who develop structured digital products reduce reliance on volatile advertising income. Products create assets. Assets create leverage. The key is clarity of transformation. When the audience understands the outcome provided, pricing becomes rational rather than emotional.

Diaspora Monetization Opportunities

The African diaspora represents a significant economic bridge. Diaspora audiences often seek cultural connection, investment insight, educational access, and partnership opportunities linked to the continent. Creators positioned strategically can serve both local and diaspora segments through differentiated offerings. Cross-border monetization reduces dependency on single-market purchasing power. It also introduces currency diversification, which protects income stability. Designing offers that resonate across markets strengthens long-term resilience.

Strategic Partnerships

Partnerships extend revenue beyond individual effort. Brands, institutions, startups, and educational entities increasingly seek credible digital voices to reach engaged communities. Strategic partnerships must be aligned with positioning and audience trust. Short-term sponsorships that undermine credibility damage long-term earning potential. Selective alignment strengthens authority and increases lifetime value. Negotiating from a position of structured influence rather than raw follower count produces stronger agreements.

Case Studies

Real-world application demonstrates possibility. African creators who diversify income beyond ad revenue consistently demonstrate stronger financial resilience. Those who combine services, digital products, community monetization, and selective partnerships outperform those relying solely on algorithm-driven income. Case studies illustrate a consistent pattern: authority plus structure equals sustainability. Visibility alone does not.

Monetization without permission is not about rejecting platforms. It is about refusing dependency. It is about building systems that function regardless of policy changes or algorithm shifts. When revenue is diversified and value is clear, independence becomes achievable.
With monetization structured, the next challenge becomes ownership and protection.

CASE STUDIES — SYSTEMS IN ACTION

Note on Case Studies: Some case studies in this section draw from publicly documented creators and platforms. Others are composite scenarios based on recurring patterns observed across African creator and business ecosystems. In composite scenarios, names and identifying details have been changed to protect privacy while preserving the strategic lessons.

Pan African Lifestyle — From Cultural Idea to Structured Multimedia Infrastructure

Pan African Lifestyle began with no audience, no funding, and no institutional backing. What existed was conviction: that Pan-Africanism could be positioned not as an abstract ideology, but as a lifestyle brand. Early feedback suggested the concept was too academic, too institutional, and not commercially viable. Instead of diluting the message, the founders structured it. Over five years, the brand built a cross-platform audience exceeding half a million followers, reaching tens of millions monthly across digital channels. In the early phase, growth required volume, with five to ten pieces of content posted daily to establish narrative presence. In the refinement phase, content volume decreased while positioning strengthened. The overarching narrative became clear: The African Dream, anchored by pillars of connection, culture, collective capital, and community. What transformed the brand was infrastructure. Books were published. Apparel lines launched. Over 190 original songs were produced. Conferences, digital tools, proprietary initiatives, and ecosystem-building efforts expanded the brand beyond content into structured enterprise. Revenue diversification replaced platform dependency. Authority replaced popularity. The lesson is structural: ideology becomes powerful when systematized. Audience growth becomes economic leverage when aligned with clear offers, recurring products, and owned infrastructure.

Wode Maya — From Viral Moment to Continental Authority

Wode Maya began without institutional power or mainstream sponsorship. What he possessed was narrative clarity. A pivotal viral moment reframed perception of Africa, challenging dominant stereotypes and showcasing lived realities. That moment generated visibility, but what sustained growth was positioning. Instead of chasing repeated virality, he built a recognizable identity around positive African storytelling. Over time, influence expanded beyond platform metrics into tourism impact, cross-border engagement, and continental recognition. The insight is critical: viral exposure is not a business model. When anchored in narrative discipline and cultural alignment, it becomes a catalyst for long-term authority.

African Stream — Platform Vulnerability and the Sovereignty Imperative

African Stream emerged as an independent African-owned multimedia platform committed to narrative sovereignty. Under the leadership of Ahmed Kaballo, the platform built ideological influence and digital traction. However, heavy reliance on external global platform infrastructure exposed structural vulnerability. When deplatforming occurred, distribution collapsed rapidly. The lesson is architectural, not emotional. No matter how strong a message becomes, dependency on external gatekeepers creates fragility. Sovereignty requires layered control: direct audience access, diversified revenue streams, and owned infrastructure.

Narrative power must be matched by structural resilience.

IShowSpeed — Narrative Disruption at Global Scale

In a 28-day multi-country Africa tour, IShowSpeed demonstrated the scale at which digital personalities can reshape perception. Broadcasting live experiences across multiple African countries exposed millions to alternative narratives, including modern infrastructure, vibrant communities, and dynamic youth culture. The impact was not merely entertainment; it shifted global perception in real time and intensified conversation around tourism and continental visibility. The strategic takeaway is clear: attention is geopolitical. When directed at scale, it becomes narrative diplomacy.

Composite Case Study — The Creator Who Went Viral but Stayed Broke

A lifestyle creator amassed hundreds of thousands of followers after a series of viral posts. Engagement surged. Visibility expanded. Revenue remained inconsistent. There was no defined offer, no email infrastructure, and no owned platform. Sponsorships were sporadic and underpriced. When algorithm changes reduced reach, income declined immediately. The turning point came when the creator restructured around clear positioning, defined value, and a structured offer. A digital product aligned with audience need was launched alongside email capture and a subscription community. Within twelve months, revenue stabilized and surpassed prior sponsorship earnings. Popularity without monetization architecture is illusion. Authority plus structured value equals sustainability.

Composite Case Study — The Diaspora Bridge Model

An entrepreneurship-focused creator built strong engagement locally but struggled with conversion due to purchasing power constraints. Instead of raising prices uniformly, the creator segmented offerings. Accessible digital tools served local markets, while higher-tier consulting and educational programs targeted diaspora audiences. Currency diversification stabilized income and reduced volatility. Monetization must reflect economic reality. Strategy replaces frustration when segmentation replaces uniform pricing.

Composite Case Study — The Operator Who Survived Deplatforming

An educational media brand relied heavily on a single social platform for distribution. When visibility dropped drastically after a policy shift, revenue collapsed. However, prior investment in email infrastructure and private community platforms allowed communication continuity. Traffic was redirected to owned channels, and revenue stabilized within months. Ownership protects momentum. Infrastructure reduces vulnerability.

Composite Case Study — From Creator to Institution

A niche creator-built authority through consistent educational content. Instead of remaining an influencer, the brand evolved into a structured entity offering certification programs, institutional partnerships, and advisory services. Over time, corporations and institutions engaged not for promotion but for strategy. Institutional influence is the natural progression of disciplined digital architecture.

Revenue is responsibility. Monetization is maturity. A creator who cannot convert value into income remains dependent on systems they do not control. Sustainable income does not come from hope. It comes from structure, clarity, and ownership. When monetization is intentional, independence becomes realistic. The next evolution is sovereignty.

PART V

PLATFORM INDEPENDENCE & DIGITAL OWNERSHIP

From Dependency to Sovereignty

Dependency is subtle. It begins when creators rely entirely on external systems for distribution, monetization, and audience access. When algorithms shift, income fluctuates. When policies change, reach declines. When platforms restrict access, growth stalls. Dependency limits strategic control. Sovereignty begins when creators design systems that function independently of any single gatekeeper. This does not require abandoning platforms. It requires reducing reliance on them. Digital sovereignty at the creator level means controlling your audience relationships, your revenue pathways, and your intellectual property.

Owning Platforms

True ownership begins with direct audience access. Email lists, membership portals, community platforms, and owned websites provide stability that social feeds cannot guarantee. When a creator owns a direct communication channel, reach is not determined solely by algorithms. Audience relationships become durable. Owned platforms create resilience. They allow creators to communicate, launch, and monetize without waiting for external permission. Platform ownership transforms temporary attention into long-term leverage.

Platforms and Data

Data is insight. Insight is power. Creators who understand audience behavior, engagement patterns, and purchasing signals can make strategic decisions. Relying solely on platform-provided metrics limits understanding. Building owned systems allows for deeper data capture and more informed optimization. Data-driven strategy reduces guesswork and increases efficiency. Ownership of data strengthens independence and improves long-term performance.

Self-Reliant Systems

Self-reliance does not mean isolation. It means stability. A self-reliant digital system integrates content production, distribution, monetization, and communication into a cohesive structure. When one channel slows, others sustain momentum. When one revenue stream fluctuates, others compensate. Self-reliant systems are diversified and aligned. They prioritize predictability over excitement. Sustainable creators design systems that continue functioning even during volatility.

Protecting Content

Intellectual property is an asset. Content, frameworks, courses, and brand identity must be protected. Clear ownership rights, licensing awareness, and contractual discipline strengthen long-term value. Many creators underestimate the importance of formal agreements and brand protection until conflicts arise. Protecting content ensures that growth translates into retained value. It transforms creative output into defensible capital.

Cybersecurity

Digital infrastructure must be secured. Account breaches, data loss, and unauthorized access can destabilize entire operations. Basic cybersecurity hygiene—strong authentication practices, secure data storage, and platform protection—prevents avoidable disruption. As revenue grows, security becomes non-negotiable. Professional digital operations require disciplined protection of systems and information.

Standards for Trust

Trust remains the core currency of digital ecosystems. Ownership without integrity erodes credibility. Transparency in partnerships, clarity in communication, and ethical monetization reinforce trust. When creators align commercial activity with audience value, long-term loyalty strengthens. Standards for trust protect reputation, and reputation protects income.

Professional Standards

Digital entrepreneurship demands professionalism. Clear communication, defined delivery timelines, structured offers, and measurable outcomes separate sustainable operators from casual participants. Professional standards elevate perception. Elevated perception increases pricing power. The move from hobbyist to structured operator is marked by operational discipline.

Transparency and Accountability

Growth amplifies scrutiny. Transparent communication about partnerships, pricing, and value builds long-term credibility. Accountability strengthens authority. When creators acknowledge responsibility for outcomes and correct mistakes openly, trust deepens. Sustainable influence depends not only on innovation but on integrity.

Scaling Influence

Scaling is not merely increasing audience size. It is expanding systems capacity. True scale occurs when infrastructure supports growth without collapsing under pressure. Delegation, automation, and strategic partnerships allow influence to expand sustainably.

Scaling requires preparation. Without structure, rapid growth creates instability. With infrastructure, growth multiplies impact. Platform independence and digital ownership shift the creator from participant to proprietor. Ownership protects income. Structure protects growth. Discipline protects reputation. When these elements align, influence becomes durable. From this foundation, expansion becomes possible beyond individual success.

Ownership changes posture. It shifts a creator from participant to proprietor. Platforms are tools, not foundations. Algorithms fluctuate, but owned systems endure. Those who control their audience relationships, revenue streams, and intellectual property cannot be easily displaced. Independence is not isolation. It is stability.

PART VI

FROM CREATOR TO CONTINENTAL IMPACT

Institutional and Personal Impact

Individual success is powerful, but institutional impact compounds. A creator who builds authority, monetization systems, and ownership infrastructure has the capacity to influence beyond personal brand visibility. Influence can shape industries, education standards, entrepreneurial ecosystems, and cultural narratives. Personal impact generates income. Institutional impact generates legacy. The transition begins when creators stop thinking only about content output and begin thinking about system contribution.

Institutional Influence

Institutional influence emerges when digital authority intersects with organizational structures. Governments, corporations, educational institutions, and startups increasingly rely on credible digital voices to interpret markets and mobilize communities. Creators who operate with discipline, clarity, and professionalism become strategic partners rather than promotional tools. Institutional influence requires credibility that extends beyond follower counts. It requires documented expertise, consistent value delivery, and operational maturity. When authority is structured, institutions respond.

Campaigns for Governments and Corporations

Digital ecosystems now shape public policy conversations, corporate reputation, and economic narratives. Creators who understand positioning can contribute meaningfully to campaigns that influence entrepreneurship, financial literacy, technology adoption, and innovation ecosystems. Structured collaboration elevates both parties. However, alignment is critical. Short-term transactional partnerships weaken authority. Long-term strategic alignment strengthens credibility and impact. Creators who operate as structured entities negotiate from strength rather than dependency.

Public-Private Partnerships

The intersection between public and private sectors presents opportunity for scalable influence. Digital creators can contribute to educational initiatives, youth empowerment programs, economic development campaigns, and innovation advocacy. Structured participation requires professional standards and operational readiness. When creators design systems that can integrate into larger initiatives, they extend their influence beyond individual monetization into structural development.

Entrepreneurial State and Private Sector

Digital influence increasingly intersects with entrepreneurship. Creators who build authority in technology, finance, education, or business sectors often evolve into founders, investors, or ecosystem builders. The line between content creation and enterprise development becomes fluid. Structured digital authority enables access to networks, capital, and strategic partnerships. When creators think entrepreneurially, they convert influence into economic infrastructure.

Financing the Digital Century

Sustainable growth requires capital literacy. As digital ecosystems expand, creators must understand investment models, funding pathways, and revenue reinvestment strategies. Financial discipline determines whether income becomes temporary consumption or long-term leverage. Structured reinvestment into infrastructure, talent, and systems strengthens competitive positioning. Financing is not limited to venture capital or institutional backing. It includes disciplined profit allocation and strategic scaling.

Investment Models

Creators who transition into operators evaluate opportunities through structured criteria. They consider sustainability, alignment, and scalability. Investment may take the form of expanding digital products, developing technology platforms, building media entities, or forming collaborative ventures. Strategic investment transforms influence into equity. Equity builds long-term wealth.

Governance and Standards

As influence grows, governance becomes necessary. Clear policies, contractual discipline, and operational transparency protect systems from internal instability. Governance is not bureaucracy. It is structured accountability. It ensures that growth does not compromise integrity. Mature digital ecosystems depend on disciplined leadership.

Measuring Influence and Impact

Impact must be measured intentionally. Surface metrics provide limited insight into structural influence. True impact is reflected in revenue stability, partnership depth, institutional collaboration, community retention, and ecosystem contribution. Measurement aligned with long-term objectives clarifies direction. It transforms ambition into strategy.

KPIs for Authority

Key performance indicators for authority extend beyond engagement statistics. They include repeat partnerships, sustained audience retention, product conversion rates, and institutional recognition. Authority measured properly becomes predictable.

Predictability strengthens leverage. Leveraged authority enables expansion.

Phased Implementation: 2030 → 2040 → 2050

Long-term thinking distinguishes participants from builders. Phased implementation recognizes that digital dominance evolves. Early phases prioritize authority and monetization. Mid phases prioritize infrastructure and institutional partnerships. Later phases prioritize ownership, investment, and ecosystem contribution. Strategic timelines prevent short-term thinking from undermining long-term impact.

Step-by-Step Roadmap

Continental impact does not begin with scale. It begins with structure. Creators must master identity, authority, attention, monetization, and ownership before expanding influence outward. Each phase builds on disciplined execution of the previous one. When systems are aligned, expansion becomes sustainable rather than chaotic.

The African digital century will not be defined solely by those who gain followers. It will be defined by those who build systems, institutions, and infrastructure that endure. Influence becomes power when it is structured. Power becomes legacy when it is disciplined. This book began with opportunity. It concludes with responsibility. Digital dominance is not accidental. It is engineered.

Individual success proves possibility. Institutional influence proves permanence. The African digital century will not be defined by those who accumulated followers. It will be defined by those who built infrastructure. Influence becomes power when structured. Power becomes legacy when disciplined.

LESSONS LEARNED

After years of building, refining, testing, failing, adjusting, and rebuilding, certain principles have proven consistent.

Visibility is rented. Ownership is built.

High reach does not guarantee high revenue. Attention without structure produces volatility. Structure converts attention into stability.

Posting more content does not create dominance. Clarity creates dominance. When identity, positioning, and value are aligned, growth compounds naturally.

Audience size is less important than audience alignment. A smaller, trusted community will outperform a large, disengaged following.

Authority grows through repetition of value. Trust grows through consistency. Revenue grows through disciplined systems.

Monetization must be intentional. Waiting for platforms to pay fairly is not a strategy. Designing offers that solve real problems is.

Diversification protects stability. Relying on one platform, one revenue stream, or one distribution channel creates fragility.

Infrastructure determines longevity. Email lists, owned platforms, intellectual property, and direct audience relationships outlast algorithm shifts.

Professional standards separate hobbyists from operators. Discipline, documentation, systems, and accountability elevate perception and increase leverage.

Influence carries responsibility. Ethical clarity protects reputation. Reputation protects revenue.

The digital economy rewards builders more than performers. Those who think long-term outlast those who chase trends.

The African digital century will not be shaped by those who accumulate followers. It will be shaped by those who build systems.

These lessons are not theoretical. They were earned through experimentation, recalibration, strategic partnerships, platform volatility, monetization challenges, and disciplined execution. They apply across markets, across platforms, and across generations.

Build deliberately.
Monetize strategically.
Own your systems.
Scale with discipline.
Contribute beyond yourself.

The future belongs to those who design it.

CONCLUSION

DESIGNING THE AFRICAN DIGITAL CENTURY

The African digital century is not a prediction. It is a construction project.

The systems that will define it are being built now — by creators, operators, entrepreneurs, educators, technologists, and institutions who understand that visibility alone is insufficient. Influence must be structured. Authority must be engineered. Revenue must be diversified. Ownership must be protected.

Throughout this book, one principle has remained constant: attention without structure is fragile. Structure without monetization is incomplete. Monetization without ownership is vulnerable.

Digital dominance is the alignment of all three.

The African Creator Power Stack™ transforms creativity into authority. The African Attention Engine™ transforms visibility into predictable growth. Monetization without permission transforms influence into income. Platform independence transforms income into sovereignty. Continental impact transforms sovereignty into legacy.

This progression is not theoretical. It is practical. It is executable. It is repeatable.

Africa's digital ecosystem will continue evolving. Platforms will shift. Technologies will change. Policies will adapt. But disciplined systems endure. Creators who build with clarity, ownership, and long-term vision will outlast algorithm cycles and trend waves.

The opportunity before this generation is significant. For the first time, influence can be built without traditional gatekeepers. Audiences can be reached directly. Knowledge can be monetized independently. Intellectual property can scale globally.

But opportunity alone does not guarantee impact.

Structure does.

Digital dominance requires responsibility. It requires ethical discipline, economic literacy, and professional standards. It requires creators to think beyond applause and toward infrastructure. It requires movement from creator to architect to operator.

The African digital century will not be defined by those who post the most content. It will be defined by those who build the strongest systems.

The choice is no longer whether Africa will participate in the global digital economy.

The choice is whether African creators will own their position within it.

Build deliberately.
Monetize strategically.
Own your systems.
Scale with discipline.

Design your influence so that it compounds.

Design your systems so that they endure.

Design your legacy so that it strengthens the continent.

The work begins now.

APPENDICES

This section must not feel like filler. It should reinforce authority and make the book feel structured, system-based, and professional. We'll write them in paragraph format, with bolded titles, clean and concise — but powerful. Here we go.

APPENDIX A – AFRICAN ATTENTION ENGINE™ MODEL MAP

The African Attention Engine™ operates as a structured flow rather than a random growth mechanism. It begins with clear positioning, which informs narrative direction and content architecture. That content feeds targeted distribution across selected platforms, which generates attention aligned with defined audiences. Structured engagement then converts attention into measurable participation, including subscriptions, inquiries, and purchases. Retention mechanisms ensure that engagement compounds rather than resets with each new post. The model emphasizes predictability over virality and long-term stability over temporary spikes. Attention is treated as an asset that must flow into authority and monetization pathways rather than dissipate into surface metrics.

APPENDIX B – PLATFORM INDEPENDENCE FRAMEWORK MAP

Platform independence is built on layered control. Distribution channels create visibility, but owned assets create stability. The framework begins with audience capture through direct communication channels such as email lists and community platforms. It integrates diversified revenue streams that do not rely on a single payout source. Data ownership strengthens strategic decision-making, while intellectual property protection secures long-term value. Infrastructure resilience ensures that operations continue even when external platforms shift policies or algorithms. The framework emphasizes controlled growth, diversified income, and secure systems as the foundation of digital sovereignty.

APPENDIX C – AFRICA 2050 DIGITAL SCORECARD

Long-term digital dominance requires measurement beyond short-term metrics. The Africa 2050 Digital Scorecard evaluates structural progress through indicators such as revenue stability, audience retention, cross-border monetization, institutional partnerships, intellectual property ownership, and reinvestment discipline. It assesses not only visibility but durability. Sustainable digital ecosystems will be defined by creators who convert influence into equity, partnerships into infrastructure, and revenue into long-term assets. The scorecard serves as a strategic reminder that growth must be evaluated against future resilience, not immediate applause.

ACKNOWLEDGMENTS

This work has been shaped by builders, mentors, and pioneers whose influence extends beyond platforms into systems, institutions, and economic transformation.

Recognition is extended to Myron Golden, a multimillionaire business growth strategist, best-selling author, and inspirational speaker who has dedicated his career to empowering entrepreneurs to achieve measurable success. His teachings on clear offers, structured systems, value creation, and scalable business models have significantly influenced the strategic foundations reflected in this work. His emphasis on disciplined monetization and principled entrepreneurship reinforces the belief that influence must be supported by sound business architecture.

Acknowledgment is also given to Wode Maya, widely regarded as Africa's most influential YouTuber and a global ambassador of the continent's narrative. Through consistent storytelling and cross-continental engagement, he has demonstrated that African creators possess both influence and global impact. His work has contributed to a paradigm shift in how Africa is perceived, particularly in tourism, entrepreneurship, and innovation. His example affirms that narrative ownership is power.

Appreciation is extended to Ahmed Kaballo, founder of African Stream and a trailblazer in African digital media. His efforts to build a pan-African digital news and storytelling platform underscore the importance of media sovereignty, narrative control, and institutional voice in the digital age.

Gratitude is further extended to Timothy Dixon and Gabriel Moore, founders of EntreBeliever and architects of multiple eight-figure digital brands. Their mentorship and instruction in execution, brand scaling, and structured digital commerce have reinforced the necessity of disciplined systems in transforming ideas into enterprise.

Each of these individuals embodies principles central to this book: clarity, ownership, structure, discipline, and impact.

Their example strengthens the conviction that the digital African century will be built not merely by presence, but by systems.

DIGITAL DOMINANCE AFRICA

How African Creators Build Audiences,
Monetize Their Work & Thrive Independently

EMMANUEL BOPE *and* SOLANGE BOPE

AUTHORS

Emmanuel Bope is a visionary entrepreneur, cultural strategist, and digital innovator whose work operates at the intersection of Pan-African identity, entrepreneurship, and global connectivity. Born in the Democratic Republic of the Congo and raised in Canada, he merges lived cultural heritage with formal expertise in branding, digital marketing, and business development.

As Co-Founder and Chief Executive Officer of Pan African Lifestyle, Emmanuel transformed a bold basement vision launched in 2020 into a global ecosystem reaching more than half a million followers worldwide. Each month, PAL content engages millions across the global Black diaspora, shaping conversations around travel, relocation, investment, culture, and economic empowerment. He is co-author of *Africa 101, Investing In Africa 101, Due Diligence Africa, Wonders of Africa, Project Africa 2050,* and *African Etiquette 101* — a strategic portfolio designed to equip diasporans and global investors with practical frameworks to navigate the continent confidently and with clarity.

Emmanuel's leadership extends beyond publishing. He has spearheaded the development of the PAL App, a digital infrastructure connecting diaspora communities to verified opportunities across the continent, and PANAFRICON, a major Pan-African conference advancing economic collaboration and cultural alignment. He is also co-creator of Mogul May, also known as Mai Magnat, an annual continental initiative and cultural movement established by Pan African Lifestyle. Positioned as a strategic counterpart to Detty December, Mogul May dedicates the month of May to investment, entrepreneurship, legacy building, and structured economic engagement across Africa, empowering both continental Africans and members of the diaspora to invest with purpose and measurable impact.

His portfolio further includes innovative cultural products such as PAL Trivia, the Umoja card game, Pan-African music projects, and identity-centered apparel lines. He holds diplomas in Public Relations and

Marketing Communications, along with a degree in Marketing Science, applying academic rigor to scalable Pan-African enterprise. His work advances a modern expression of The African Dream rooted in ownership, preparation, and sustainable prosperity.

Solange Bope is an entrepreneur, creative director, and brand strategist whose leadership blends African heritage with contemporary innovation in design, digital media, and cultural storytelling. Born in the Democratic Republic of the Congo and raised in Canada, she co-founded Pan African Lifestyle in 2020 with a mission to make Pan-Africanism aspirational, practical, and globally accessible.

As President of PAL, Solange has defined the organization's creative vision and brand architecture. From concept to execution, she helped build PAL into a multidimensional platform spanning publishing, digital media, apparel, games, music, and community infrastructure. She is co-author of *Africa 101, Investing In Africa 101, Due Diligence Africa, Wonders of Africa, Project Africa 2050*, and *African Etiquette 101* — works that provide education, structure, and strategic clarity for the diaspora seeking deeper engagement with the continent.

She is also co-creator of Mogul May, helping shape it into a recognized continental movement that repositions May as a season of economic activation, partnership, and legacy creation across Africa. Solange holds diplomas in Fashion Styling, Image Consulting, and Marketing Communications, which she integrates into brand strategy, storytelling, and experiential design across PAL's ventures. Her expertise lies in building culturally grounded yet globally competitive brands that celebrate identity while advancing economic empowerment.

Together, Emmanuel and Solange lead Pan African Lifestyle Inc., pioneering initiatives that bridge tradition and innovation while strengthening economic pathways between Africa and its global diaspora. Through publishing, technology, live convenings, cultural movements such as Mogul May, and scalable enterprise infrastructure, they continue shaping a new era of structured engagement, ownership, and excellence aligned with The African Dream.